A Scottish Folk Tale

The
Tiny, Tiny BOY
and the
Big, Big
COW

by Nancy Van Laan

pictures by
Marjorie Priceman

Dragonfly Books® Alfred A. Knopf · New York

A NOTE ABOUT THE TEXT: *The Tiny, Tiny Boy and the Big, Big Cow* is an adaptation of a Scottish folk tale—*The Wee, Wee Mannie and the Big, Big Coo*—which was retold in *More English Fairy Tales*, compiled by Joseph Jacobs and published in 1894. Mr. Jacobs's source was Mrs. Balfour, an avid collector of English folk tales, who was first told the story by her Scottish nurse.

DRAGONFLY BOOKS® PUBLISHED BY ALFRED A. KNOPF, INC.

Text copyright © 1993 by Nancy Van Laan
Illustrations copyright © 1993 by Marjorie Priceman

www.randomhouse.com/kids

Library of Congress Cataloging-in-Publication Data
Van Laan, Nancy.
The tiny, tiny boy and the big, big cow / by Nancy Van Laan ; illustrated by Marjorie Priceman.
p.   cm.
Summary: A cumulative story in which a tiny, tiny boy tries to milk a big, big cow who will not stand still.
[1. Cows—Fiction.] I. Priceman, Marjorie, ill. II. Title.
PZ7.V3268Ti   1993
[E]—dc20   91-33738

ISBN 0-375-80478-1 (pbk.)

First Dragonfly Books® edition: March 2000

Printed in the United States of America
10 9 8 7 6 5 4 3 2 1

For Malka,
my best, best mentor and
my good, good friend
—NVL

For Jean and Jonathan
—MP

The
Tiny, Tiny BOY
and the
Big, Big
COW

A tiny, tiny boy had a big, big cow.
When he went out to milk her,
she would not stand still.
"Oh, no!" said the tiny, tiny boy.
"What shall I do now,
with this big, big cow?"
So he went to tell his ma.

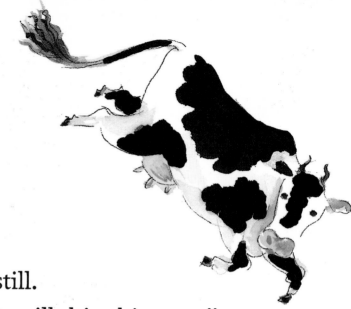

"Ma," said he,
"cow won't stand still.
Tiny, tiny boy can't milk big, big cow."
"Humph," said his ma.
"Go tell that cow
she **must** stand still."

So off went the tiny, tiny boy
to the big, big cow and said,
"Big, big cow can't have her way!
She **must** stand still.
Stand still, I say!"
But the big, big cow
kicked up her hard, hard heels
and would not stand still.

"Ma," groaned the tiny, tiny boy,
"big, big cow won't stand still.
Tiny, tiny boy can't milk big, big cow."
"Humph," said his ma.
"Get a fat, fat stick.
Shake it at that cow."

So off he went
with a fat, fat stick,
shook it at the big, big cow and said,
"Big, big cow, you **must** stand still
or my fat, fat stick I'll make you feel!"
But the big, big cow
kicked up her hard, hard heels,
swished her long, long tail,
and would not stand still.

"Ma," cried the tiny, tiny boy,
"I told the big, big cow she **must**.
I shook the fat, fat stick,
but she won't stand still.
Tiny, tiny boy can't milk big, big cow."
"Humph," said his ma.
"Get my golden gown of silk
to coax that cow."

So off he went
with the golden gown of silk,
laid it down on the ground and said,
"Hold still, big, big cow.
Fill my bucket full of milk
and then I'll let you wear
this golden gown of silk."
But the big, big cow
kicked up her hard, hard heels,
swished her long, long tail,
tossed her empty, empty head,
and would not stand still.

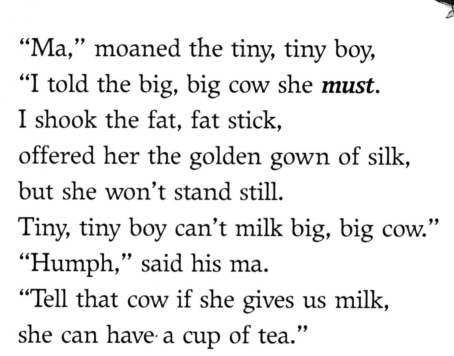

"Ma," moaned the tiny, tiny boy,
"I told the big, big cow she **must**.
I shook the fat, fat stick,
offered her the golden gown of silk,
but she won't stand still.
Tiny, tiny boy can't milk big, big cow."
"Humph," said his ma.
"Tell that cow if she gives us milk,
she can have a cup of tea."

So off he went
with a teapot and two cups
to the big, big cow and said,
"Big, big cow, please listen to me.
If you give us milk, you can have a cup of tea."
But the big, big cow
kicked up her hard, hard heels,
swished her long, long tail,
tossed her empty, empty head,
dropped her sharp, sharp horns,
and would not stand still.

"Ma," wept the tiny, tiny boy,
"I told the big, big cow she **must**.
I shook the fat, fat stick,
offered her the golden gown of silk,
and invited her to tea,
but she won't stand still.
Tiny, tiny boy can't milk big, big cow."
"Humph," said his ma.
"Go to that cow
and warm her cold, cold heart.
Tell her a sweet, sweet kitten
is crying for her milk."

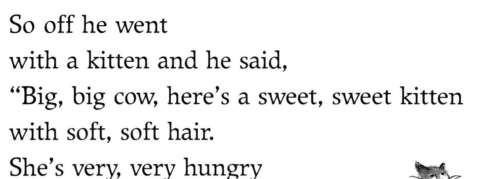

So off he went
with a kitten and he said,
"Big, big cow, here's a sweet, sweet kitten
with soft, soft hair.
She's very, very hungry
and hopes that you care.

You would cry in this bucket
if only you would think.
She's moaning and she's groaning
for a drop of milk to drink."
But the big, big cow
kicked up her hard, hard heels,
swished her long, long tail,
tossed her empty, empty head,
dropped her sharp, sharp horns,
wobbled her knobby, knobby knees,
and would not stand still.

"Ma," wailed the tiny, tiny boy,
"I told the big, big cow she **must**.
I shook the fat, fat stick,
offered her the golden gown of silk,
and invited her to tea.
I showed the sweet, sweet kitten,
but she won't stand still.
Tiny, tiny boy can't milk big, big cow."
"Humph," said his ma.
"Go to that cow!
This time you tell her
SHE MUST **NOT** STAND STILL!"

So off he went with nothing
and said,
"Big, big cow, DON'T YOU *DARE* STAND STILL!"
And the big, big cow
kicked up her hard, hard heels,
swished her long, long tail,
tossed her empty, empty head,
dropped her sharp, sharp horns,
wobbled her knobby, knobby knees,
bellowed out loudly, "MOO-O-OO!"
and...

at last stood still!